Cello Time Runners

T0086899

Piano accompaniment book

Kathy and David Blackwell

Contents

1.	Start the show	2
3.	Heat haze	4
4.	Medieval tale	5
5.	Chase in the dark	6
6.	Spy movie	7
7.	Gypsy dance	8
9.	On the go!	9
10.	That's how it goes!	10
11.	Blue whale	12
12.	Mean street chase	13
13.	Allegretto (Mozart)	14
14.	Cornish May song	15
16.	Prelude from 'Te Deum' (Charpentier)	16
17.	Paris café	17
18.	Starry night	18
19.	Cello Time rag	20
20.	Caribbean sunshine	22
21.	Jacob's dance	23
22.	Song from the show	24
23.	The road to Donegal	26
24.	Cat's eyes	28
25.	Mexican fiesta	30
26.	Summer evening	31
27.	Extension rock	32
28.	Show off!	33
30.	One day	34
31.	Aerobics	35
32.	Hungarian folk dance	36
33.	Show stopper	38
34.	Farewell to Skye	40

MUSIC DEPARTMENT

OXFORD
UNIVERSITY PRESS

1. Start the show

(for Clare)

KB & DB

Rock tempo

The cello book contains several cello duets; these are unaccompanied and so not included here.

© Oxford University Press 2002 and 2014

Printed in Great Britain

OXFORD UNIVERSITY PRESS, MUSIC DEPARTMENT, GREAT CLARENDON STREET, OXFORD OX2 6DP

The Moral Rights of the Composers have been asserted. Photocopying this copyright material is ILLEGAL.

16
mp cresc.
mp cresc.
2
19
f
f
mf
mf
22
f
f
26

3. Heat haze

KB & DB

4. Medieval tale

KB & DB

5. Chase in the dark

KB & DB

6. Spy movie

KB & DB

7. Gypsy dance

KB & DB

9. On the go!

KB & DB

* The repeat is written out in full in the cello part.

10. That's how it goes!

KB & DB

13
16
mp
mp
19
cresc.
cresc.
D.C. al Fine
22
f
f

11. Blue whale

KB & DB

12. Mean street chase

KB & DB

13. Allegretto

Mozart

14. Cornish May song

Traditional

16. Prelude from 'Te Deum'

Charpentier

17. Paris café

KB & DB

18. Starry night

KB & DB

19
23
poco rit.
a tempo
dim.
mp
dim.
mp
27
32
rall.
dim.
p
dim.
p

19. Cello Time rag

KB & DB

17
f
f
21
mp
mp
25
29
mf
mf
33
cresc.
f
cresc.
f

20. Caribbean sunshine

KB & DB

21. Jacob's dance

KB & DB

22. Song from the show

KB & DB

13
mf
mf
16
f
cresc.
f
19
rall.
a tempo
mf
dim.
mp
mf
dim.
mp
22
V
pizz.
f
f

23. The road to Donegal

KB & DB

Can also be bowed: ♩ ♪ ♩ ♪ | etc.

17
f
p
21
f
p
25
f
29

24. Cat's eyes

KB & DB

21
arco
f
f
26
31
pizz.
p
mf
p
36
arco
ff
ff

25. Mexican fiesta

KB & DB

26. Summer evening

KB & DB

27. Extension rock

KB & DB

28. Show off!

KB & DB

30. One day

KB & DB

31. Aerobics

KB & DB

32. Hungarian folk dance

KB & DB

21
mp
x4
1
mp
27
f
f
33
p
39
2nd time accelerando
mf (ff)
mf (ff)
43
1.
2.
ff
ff

33. Show stopper

KB & DB

20
24
ff
x4
2
f
ff
f
29
ff
mf
mp
cresc.
ff
mf dim.
mp
34
cresc.
mf
p
mp
cresc.
40
cresc.
f
ff
mf
cresc.
f
ff

34. Farewell to Skye

(for Iain)

KB & DB